Sirenland

Jennifer Barone

Sirenland, by Jennifer Barone
First Edition

Copyright © 2026 by Jennifer Barone

Edited by Ingrid Keir
Artwork and design by Jennifer Barone
Photography by Jennifer Barone & Daniel Heffez

ISBN-13: 978-0-9860231-3-2

Published by Feather Press, Petaluma, CA
featherpressbooks.wordpress.com

For more information, please contact the publisher at:
featherpressinfo@gmail.com

Sirenland

Jennifer Barone

For my mother *Maryann,*

la nostra famiglia, and

the Blessed Mother

who watches over us

Sea Creatures

Reasons to Return

Sirenland

Canzone

I hear the song
of my grandmothers
when I wander
the edge of the sea

Rosa, powerful rose
Anna, mother of grace
Consiglia, great advisor
Angelina, little angel

waiting
for a willing ear
their voices echo
in dark sea caverns
when I dream

those who understand
hear their song

it cuts as deep
as the crevasse
in your heart will follow
in rhythm with the waves

passage through
a vast ocean
that births stars

Creation

once I was an egg
inside my mother
inside my grandmother

we swam
in a watery continuum
initiated by the love song
of our mother

one sang, a sea inside of her
one submerged, sustained by a snake
one an egg, waiting to become
daughter, mother, grandmother
I would meet only in dreams

we shed our forms
when she hummed
the melody of our blood
in heart rhythms
rubbed her belly in spirals
music of the spheres
spun in flowers
and figure eights

she sang the story
when we lived in grottos
before crossing the ocean
we drank from her breast
nourished by the dark
in a bottomless blue

remember
we emerged
to break the pattern
to return the wild part inside
alive and unafraid to sing

How to Hear Siren Songs

her song
not always melodious
often wild
incoherent

her moods
revealed in moon phases
might be deadly
may pierce your organs
repair what's misunderstood

her nature commands
live freely
enter the sea
submerge your eyes and ears
become one with a body of water

find her
guiding star in the storm
seamstress
who threads a new story
baker molding bodies
into loaves of bread
winged mother
flies through dimensions
searches for missing soul parts

her wisdom song
emerges from caverns

put your ear
against a shell
close your eyes
and listen
to your blood

Sirenland

her longing winds
between the cliffs
at dusk
cries wash upon the shore
throb against volcanic sand
recessed tides reveal
coral fingers expand
into the underworld

return to the Tyrrhenian
let my tail unfurl cerulean
until I become the sea
subject to the ebb and flow
of moon desires

her body is a city
where poetry nurtures fire
somber ashes sprout a lemon tree
a ripe tomato, a tender grape

I come from *Partenope*
my blood runs hot
my fins, cold
I breathe from gills
at night, I grow wings

swim the water's edge
let her milk nurture you
let it stoke a fire
beneath the caldera

subterranean, volcanic flesh
can dance between
woman, fish and bird

dell'Ovo

she holds the egg
she is the egg
her body its soil
she who builds
who dances
bird woman
when women were sirens
who swam the bay
of Santa Lucia

mystic eyes
grant third eye vision
pass between thresholds
the siren's egg still hides
inside Castel dell'Ovo
a glass amphora
under a spell

her primordial watery seed
swings from the shafters
of her trembling body
keeps the city safe
from volcanic eruptions

pure and powerful egg
in the healer's hands
rolls softly over skin
its delicate shell
lifts *the eye*
coaxes you to fruition
on feast days
hen feathers
sprinkle holy water
dipped in oil
bless your brow

feathers still float
in watery coves
where siren songs
beat upon the shore
ricordi, remember
where you come from
remember who
you come from

DNA Test

would it name
fourteen generations
of longing in my bones
multi-dimensional hands
reach across the sea
hairs stand on end
when I smell coffee grinds
percolating in the basement

would it intertwine
strands of knotted bread
a seven-layer cookie
of desire I don't understand
Fibonacci's sequence of bones
my hands sign language

would they decode the imprint
songs sung from balconies
aroma of anise, licorice and fennel
explain the wild look in my eyes
patterns of ache
origin of sorrow
in heart chambers
thumbs, beats
a fist against a wooden table
hands clap to keep time
thermal waters weep
from tired eyes

steam pumps a ship across the ocean
a foghorn announces its passage
ancient waters carve a spiral path
cobalt blue
winding song
of my blood

Corallini

we cross ourselves
before diving underwater
mutter prayers to sirens
beneath the waves

when light hits the surface
we descend
in coves that push and pull
in search of coral
for amulets and talismans

naked branches
hidden in pockets
held to the chest
carved into sea nymphs
and women with
flowers in their hair

pendants rest
between breasts
above the heart
vibrant crimson
resembles passion
belly of the volcano
underworld rivers
lead into the sea

when we fold our hands
to ask for blessings
fiery fingers
reach for us
from the depths
toward heaven

When I Pray

I light a candle
ask for my grandmothers
to surround me, hold me close

I find myself
in the middle of a private *festa*
a love procession
around a tree, upon a hill

they protect me
but their passions are fierce
in a moment they switch
from smiling to scolding
pull my hair
pinch my cheek till it turns pink
circle me like a wild wind

we pray to the blessed mother
who comes when they cook
to make sure the sauce comes out okay
when they worry
where their children are at night
afraid as they board a ship
or an airplane lifting
from the roots of her belly
over an expanse of sea

we are never alone
the nonni are here
they wonder why I don't call
their fingers worn from work
brow creases and mouth lines
carved from sorrow and laughter

in dreams, they open a drawer
show me photographs
a long line of faces belongs to me
names I do not know yet
great uncles and cousins
written in my bones

when I feel lost
they say, *you're here too*

they ask me to return
to the space where nothing exists
yet everyone exists
waiting to tell their stories

L'albero

in my blood
a fig, olive and lemon tree
linked arms and feet
of dancing *nonne*
circle in ecstatic frenzy
pounding drums
clicking castanets
terra, green land
sangue, blood
in flying ribbons
their voices crescendo
sweat and laughter
tremble the heavens
open a portal
we travel
toward reaching leaves
angels arrive
down deep roots
mythic beings appear
half serpent, fish and bird
when sun and moon
heighten
they pull my body
anoint my ankles
grow wings
we travel in dreams to
the feast of the Madonna
wild stars in her hair
rose petals fly
in spirals on the wind

In the Grotto

long ago we slept in grottos
stone belly of the earth
    pregnant with our bodies
watched the sea enter
nourishing milk dripped
    from stalactites
we sang to the ocean, our voice
echoed among cavernous walls
we asked for healing dreams
    in spirit realms
inside fleshy wombs, we died again
    painted ourselves red
swam in a warm ocean of stars
unable to know what form
we would become
we curled into
    galaxy whirlpools
    of a mollusk shell
    painted ammonite
a snake spiraled 'round our feet
whispered secrets
only the earth could tell
poems emerged like seedlings
that broke the dark coat of spring

My Island is a Siren

white and rugged
    she juts into the sky
    reaches for heaven
the moon illuminates
    cobalt creases of her torso
lovers kiss in the dark
    on the back of mopeds
under café tables
    a hand climbs warm thighs
      the heights of Monte Solaro
    shivers under white linen
she reclines in the sea
    where distant boats bump like bodies
her breath a hot *scirocco*
    comforts or devours
      casts engulfing mists
        that separate us from the world
a gentle tide reveals
    mother of pearl, twisted coral
      in the rosy crevice of her grotto
lips carry sea salt
hands move like a wave
    down the small of a back
a sharp crack echoes
    on cobblestone trails
      when naked toes
        lose leather sandals
a universe sparkles
    in boutique windows
lemons dangle from leaves
    bulbous glow of gold coins
      ready to be squeezed
limoncello flows around
    dangerous curves of her breasts
where Virgin Mary levitates
    forever praying for your safety

as you hang off a cliff
	carving switchbacks of a snake
infinite pleasure is found
	in aphrodisiac shells
lingers on forks
	at the end of the day
your angel hair smells of seaweed
the air thick with sex
	in her hidden places
she lulls you into azure chambers
lapis caverns echo a sigh
	against the ceiling of her mouth
on the street, wine glasses talk
cappuccino eyes peer into you
tell you to forget
	your human origins
		on her rocky shore
you are also the sea
	born from a shell in her cove
		sacrificed from heaven
a falling star
	lovers wish upon

Sleeping on Vesuvio

how can I sleep upon
your body churning with fire
        my heart accelerates
        skin begins to flush

on approach, I feel afraid
but upon you I dream
        of water and fire touching
the delicate tail of a fish
        beats upon my skin

you appear to rest
yet wildflowers
        burst on your arms
red valerian, *ginestra*
        explosive joy returns
        to the earth of my body

I wake at 3 a.m.
        to feel your heat
        spiral under my bed
creation and destruction
        beats beneath my skin
the Pleiades pulse
        above the terrace

I don't want to be dormant
        my insides are on fire
I want my dreams
        made real
as ancient lava
solidified on the flanks
        in fields of light

Vesuvio

infinite fire
the mounds of my body
golden orbs of lemon
fields of wild poppy
hills of igneous and olive
fire stirs the cavern of my belly
hidden under grapevines
I face heaven
tremble in small crescendos
dream, wide awake
under silent constellations
we will not die with feelings
that ache for release
I explode unspoken words
pressure of desire pops and wails
ashes into the firmament
syllables erupt in a sonic boom
rearranges you in a posture of tears
I am a volcano of ancestral desires
create continents
where fire and water meet
coral red, obsidian
my visceral touch
a perfume of roses and rosemary
ripple in ecstatic waves
stillness before the eruption
to live upon fiery fields
when will they devour you
subconscious rises
sirens expound their wisdom
fuming snake tendrils
we bathe in furious heat
encapsulated in ecstasy
the crown of my head
fireworks in the night
I will bury the world
under the rubble and ash
of my longing

Left Behind

hero tales never speak
    of women as casualties
the invisible
    who wear no medals
        who have no name

women
    who come on waves
        cradling children
sea foam apparitions
    on lonely ships
        over stormy seas
homes left burning
    in a wake of fire

we are never told
    women are the sea itself
the ocean is also a mother
    carrying us in her water
        nurtures us

we are never told
    we are made of water
that water holds memory
    stories of our families
        and their dreams

although they say
    leave no man behind
women and children
    are often left
        their stories untold

water holds them
    in its flow
tears rise from the sea
    fall upon mountains
run through rivers
    never stopping

Rosa

Nonno paced under your balcony
    watched you, captivated
in the evening when sunlight
    cast magenta over the volcano

what color were you wearing
    when you fell in love
the soft flush of petals

I imagine you
    carved a cameo
    like the one you left me
not far from the Madonna
    who stopped the lava
her feast day my birthday

I imagine he brought musicians
    sang you love songs
I've learned even men can be sirens
    lure you across the ocean
lead you far from home

I return to rolling hills of
    festival flowers and coral
ancient temples cultivate rose
    sacred rituals by the sea

I turn rose petals
into oil on my kitchen table
a photo of you in Sunset Park
when you brought me
to your rose garden
to smell the spinning nebula
    of infinite desire
a thousand unfolding petals

Inheritance

my grandfather's funeral
photos of men and women
dressed in black

sorrow lives inside my laughter
lingers after joy
a shadow reveals itself
in the eyes, in passing faces

crumbling ruins
streets paved with ethereal gold
cries of passion emerge from balconies
under windows, voices ascend
chatter of espresso cups at the bar
ache in my bones

you sing, a sea bird
penetrate, a sea urchin
instill a longing for paradise
in my belly, between legs
love, lightning bolts up my spine
an island view from your grave
acute ache at my crown
wants to ascend
but stays close to Earth
lives in cobblestones of the ancient port
lava through my veins

lovers cry, converse with the moon
wander to the lapping sea
thieves whip
around a corner on a moped
rob your memory
squeeze lemon on your wounds
twirl your hair like Medusa
between fingers

my heart beats an irregular rhythm
runs on virgin olive oil
the raw fire of my grandfather's
chestnut eyes, stares through mine
bleached, coral bones
reach through waves to touch you
longing hangs on the end
of every joyful sentence

where he returned to die
I ache for something more
our dreams echo into the
black and silent cosmos
    Nonno, do you know
      that sudden sigh so well?

The Mourners

we will not have women dressed in black
> no cry will pierce your chest
you're only allowed to think of the good times
> now, there will be no tears

the decadence of being able to
> mourn in public
now, only permitted
in the cold silence of your room

in Napoli
mourners entered with a moan
followed my grandfather's body
in a glass carriage through the streets
wild cries gave permission
to shed uninhibited grief

the departed
need a sufficient wave of tears
to cross the river to the next life

I carry an ocean inside
everyone can cross
unbridled gestures of despair
wild songs of praise

your porcelain portrait
watches from across the bay
where sirens leap from marble
wings outspread like angels
circulate your grave

I lament with the dead
a macabre dance on cobblestones
in dreams, siren songs crescendo
       in ecstatic exaltation

is spirit flesh or just bone?
a body washed with wine
preserved in mausoleums
a relic that liquifies on time
        guarantees a miracle

What to Do with Your Tears

separate your memories into salt
the alchemists transform

prove we drift like
constellations across the water

memories carried in a sea womb
swim with Melusine fins

dance in figure eights
appear in dreams

a great lament
returns at nightfall

I swim alone
in the sea walls of my bed

festivals of joy and sorrow
arrive in terrifying crescendos

ecstatic songs
pierce limestone cliffs

soften your edges
ferry you across stories

in the wake of their passage
propel you through ethereal waters

necessary cries
no glass container left
to collect them

don't hold back
your sacred, milky tears

let them course through you
    fill the crescent bay
nourish the ocean
    that bleeds from you

What Do Stars Look Like
in the Middle of the Ocean?

are the waves calm
placid without wind
violent as you charge
through crashing waves
of past and future selves

in the middle of the ocean
many things are hidden
the wind may stop
all directions, possible
the world is seamless, borderless
in a dark silence
you can hear your wish
blaze across the sky
fall into the sea

the wind sings
heart pounds
like waves against a ship
heavy swells carry the dreams
of all who pass

at night, all things
are made of starlight
a woman whose shoulders
sprout wings when she sleeps
whose legs become fins

past the surface
deeper in the trench
where heartbreak splits you open
no sound beyond breath
that can't encompass the cosmos

beyond the ocean floor
a quiet, soft emerging
there, the molten blood
thicker than water

Ecstasy

We Come from Pleasure

ancestral bodies
    writhe in ecstasy
on cavernous walls
    in mosaics
carved into coral
    my hair
adorned with flowers
the Pompeiian profile
    looks to the future
toward an expanding sea
    blood drips vitality
thermal water
    the *Grande Dea*
pours hot, joyful tears
    from the dark temple
light bursts forth singing
    ecstatic music of our blood
speaks over each other
    dances in the *piazza*
    on feast days
links arms, feet
    and red threads
we were made from
a passionate spark
    emerge from love
embody the pleasure vehicle
    reclaim it full of roses
dripping grapes
cornucopia of breasts
    overflows embroidered fabric
volcanic hips tremble
    lips leave devotional offerings
from cheek to cheek exclaim
    we are here for joy

How to Make Love to a Siren

if you win her favor
she may choose not to eat you
but to mingle instead

you must sing
song of the spheres
read poems
cast from constellations

then like a grotto
hidden in a wall of limestone
her tail will split in two, and you
simultaneously enter and emerge
where it's salty and warm

hot, pink magma
rises from volcanic flesh
sunlight will reveal
glowing, blue, electric blood
at her fins, now feet

the cavernous baths
embrace you
little fish
nip your skin underwater
small, love bites

Vulgare

colloquial voice of the people
words spoken in *dialetto*

you must be careful
how you use that word, she says
you don't want to be vulgar
but maybe *I do,* sometimes

street music on the *Spaccanapoli*
a man plays a melodica
steps on a rubber chicken
and makeshift foot pedals

another man sings opera
in the alcove of an ancient building
spray painted with graffiti
near Teatro San Carlo

you've never seen *this before*
never heard it said *that way*
never tasted something *quite like this*

the heart of the people
rough around the edges
on boisterous side streets
and aging corridors
they tell me not to walk through
I wander anyway
towns they tell me
to stay away from, I visit
take the train
they say is dangerous
to excavate my heart of longing
in places people want me to forget

sacred sites with
ancient, overlooked weeds
still carry medicine
sirens have a sense of humor
a little scaly
sharp toothed
their power palpable
in buried temples
on an ancient peninsula
in the ghostly shape of a fin

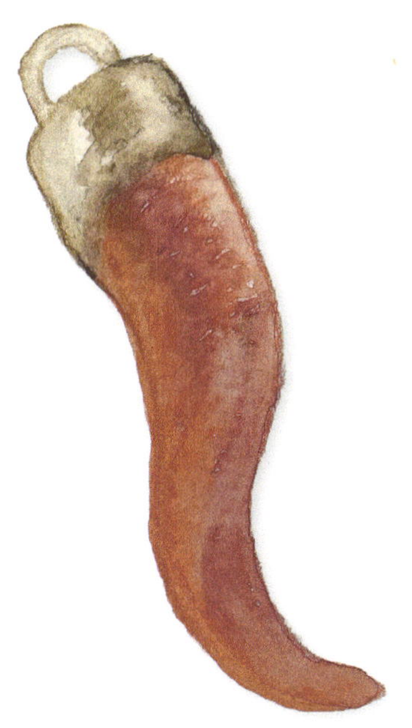

L'occhio

what cannot be seen pervades
eyes that eat good fortune forget
those who move in swift reverence

eyes see through walls
painted faces gaze from stone
fisheyes spin underwater visions
portal eyes perceive

occhi protect
purify your eyes with milk
concoct an innocuous eye
with innocence

return to the garden
naked, trembling
turn your gaze from envy
block invisible lasers
with *cornicelli* of coral
between your breasts
secret hand signals
redirect your gaze under tables

tintinnabulum over doorway
ring siren tails
sprigs of rue dangle
crescent moons and keys

tap bundles of rosemary
against the belly to clear
compliments that veil discontent
create headaches
adoring eyes
house sorrow, deflect

trespassing eyes
run wild in the street
now on screens, uncontained

power down
only open to eyes
plucked onto plates of Santa Lucia
heavenly eyes hold light within them
ask for winged mother
angels to descend
plunge an iron scissor
into oily eyes in the watery void
l'occhi never stick
once they're recognized

may they burst into pieces

Matermania

on your morning walk
you come upon voices
singing prophecies to the sun
a frenzied hexameter

golden rays illuminate
the womb of *Matermania*
rhythmic waves crash at her feet

her nymphaeum
holds hypnotic cries
infusing cobalt water
through limestone walls
gathers in whirlpools below

bodies move like waves
inside her belly
reborn with the sun
burned into the altar
naked arms reach
with starfish fingers
pushing back the dark night's
emerging stars

when the full-bodied goddess
ascends from her shell
in trembling, vulnerable flesh
she hangs from the wild cliff
in bright bursts of *ginestra*
sweet marjoram and thyme
her haunting, feverish song
liberated from the cliffs

Nymphaeum

what can I bring
to thank you for the water
cleansing my mind with rosemary
clearing my heart as it pours over me

water travels deep
from the core of earth to surface
what can I bring you
for this fire and water

I thank you with my body
add my tears
salty outpour of the spring
all spectrums of light shower me
rotating colors and geometries

nymphs are present in the sun
wings outstretched around my shoulders
soft grass offers ethereal tenderness
sweet air caresses me as I walk
wafting lavender, sage, and lemon

how can I reveal what is subtle and unseen
or sing what is quietly being whispered
when the breeze speaks
we are blessed by the land
recognized for the resonance of presence
the pleasure of our body restored

this memory lasts so long
leaves me wondering
how can I thank you?

Secret Cabinet

closed for a hundred years
open again
excavate your inhibitions
    permanently
great stone phalluses
reach for heaven
    fascinus
a woman in ecstasy
writhes above you
voyeuristic animals revolve
orgies on a wine vessel
now hidden in the
    gabinetto segreto
when they used to
bake in the sun without shame
at the curve of a courtyard
by a fountain
in the herb garden

my body does not know the word
    obscene
denies the concept of *sin*
I rewrite history with my tongue
the lost dialect of ancestors
buried in ashes of sacred sex
fluid, vital and protective

if you harness the courage
to skirt the volcanic entry
place your desire on the caldera
make offerings on the kitchen altar
you will know
    this peppered mouth is not a sin
    but a sacrament

a river of fire melts into the sea
creates a new world
with our longing

The Dancers of Villa Cicero

stop what you're doing
let yourself rest for the day
sprawl out in the sun
your eyes need rejuvenation
your heart longs to be filled
let the dancer
fly from her fresco
to spiral around you

let her enter you
roses in her hair
basket of fragrant petals
let her lift your spirit
if it needs lifting
let her bless your worker's hands
with ethereal warmth
carry you far
when your eyes close
leaving rooms and
screens of light behind

as darkness
enters to repair you
let your body rest on the earth
join her
circle galaxies
a wild angel
lit by the sound of drums
lose your sorrow
in the still point
where timelines spin
your rhythm accelerates

remember
you are alive and vital
pay attention
when the dancers
surround you in the vastness
receive what your heart needs
to feel light again

Priapus in the Night Garden

mysterious, mischievous things
happen in a garden, among fig trees
in ultraviolet light

at the edge of dusk
magenta fades into a deepening blue
pinpricks of stars reveal you
towering over me

unable to comprehend your magnitude
I realize I need to release
all limits on ecstasy
now, I think we deserve it
just for showing up
alive and willing

I didn't know I needed healing
this was not
the medicine I was expecting
could I take it all in
the god of plenty, protective vitality

the heavenly ladder is enormous
how can I climb into the void
I may never return from
explosive love
undulating peaks
hide a little death
a supernova in its frequency
leaves a black hole
devouring in its wake

loving you may tear me apart
I'm at the age where
it's time to unlearn all I've learned

why am I here?
is it possible you are
leaping from murals into flesh?

holding me until I dream again
upon waking
I am filled with insatiable desires
only fulfilled by the divine
in a heavenly garden of delight

my skin is on fire
my body
an electric wave

Cibo Cattivo

eating virgin cakes
shaped like breasts
zizzona mozzarella
bouncy *bufula* nipples
crusty snakes
eat their own tail
we ingest infinite wisdom
sacred body of bread
held on the tongue
an eternal moment
to taste knowledge
experience
with five senses
sacrifice
the density of life
on our fingers
Sant'Agata's breasts
filled with *marzipane*
dotted with cherries
tricolore pricks of angels
pussies made of pasta
the nipples of Venus
are bon bons
and what to say
about *salami*
warm chestnuts
the fertile egg
milk pours from
maternal fountains
a fertility festival
inside the mouth
an agricultural orgy
in front of clergy
the virility of *cannoli*
filled with creme
inseminating spring
alchemy of luminous time
enters us into ecstasy

Genius Loci

I press my cheek
against your grass
sand and stone
a blossoming petal
your balmy wind caresses me
I float in the warm
lapping waves of your siren cove
weightless and held

I fall asleep to your lullaby
of gurgling pebbles
sea bird cries release me
from unnamable longing
an insatiable hunger

I search for relief
in a bowl of pasta
a man's arms
a safe place to rest
but only you satiate me
it's you, that I long for
the mother who
loves without condition
embraces without pain
welcomes my tears
with tenderness
never abandons me
in the dark

you hold me
cradle me forever
like a babe
after nourishing milk
pressed against her softness
drifts into ecstasy

We Need Magic

I do not want to live in a world
that does not believe in miracles
who fails to recognize a direct line
of communion with saints
that doesn't dream of strange animals
who can't talk to apparitions or angels

all night I speak with the dead
hear my father laugh when I close my eyes
speak Italian with *nonna* in dreams
visiting a grave opens a portal
instantaneous phone calls
from family around the globe

we don't need a boat
we can astral plane
over a great silence
in the middle of the ocean

I do not want to live in a place
that does not believe
eyes can bless or curse
illness is cured by
olive oil and prayer

the unseen requires imagination
spirit needs a random act to communicate
to learn Italian is to learn surrealism
we need eyes in the feet
eyes in the hands
eyes in the back of our heads

all day I dance with the dead
relatives known and unknown
invite them to dinner
to understand how I know
the pasta is ready just by looking at it

our ancestors sing
we carry out their wishes
to remember all they lost
all we gained
even though
you're alone in your room
everyone is here
you are never alone

Blessed Mother

they say the smell of roses
marks her presence
surrounds your body
instant ascension

her heart is on fire
three arrows pierce her flesh
my heart is heavy with sorrow
anger without a safe place to go
compression that may cause eruption

she burns the frayed edges
until I remember who I am
sacred fire in the grotto of her ribs

she builds her sanctuary in a cavern
a quiet ache between shoulders
sends her message in passing thoughts
enters the steady flow of blood

she appears where lightning strikes
reveals a wooden statue
under oak or myrtle
Madonna la Bruna, the mountain
Madonna Nera, black obsidian
blazing meteorite from stars
in a painting, she is the mineral
ochre, cadmium, lapis lazuli
her eyes follow you

Madonna of the rivers and springs
coral that waves underwater
tears penetrate ceramic and stone
her sorrow mirrors yours

asks you to change your life
to climb a mountain
return to transform your tears
add them to the river
awaken her shrine with
the elements of your body
Madonna of the fingers and toes
our lady of the eyes and lips
she asks you to sing from them
exalt your heavy sigh

I don't mind the swords that pierce her flesh
tears of blood dripping from her eyes
I've collected wounds of my own now
growing from the crevice starved of water
eyes hold movements of the sea

where I grew scars
appear mystic roses and their fragrance
a growing flame emerges
where my heart breaks

Sea
Creatures

Siren

who knows when
the bird woman became a fish
her song, a mourning cry
accompanies souls to the afterlife

who said her voice
was meant to devour men
half woman, half beast
wild banshee, ready to explode
volcanic tempest
misunderstood Medusa

here, mystic statues cry and bleed
waves crash upon unruly shores
a winged woman with a fishtail
enters the underworld
dark as a meteorite
that fell from seven stars

rocky, toothsome, dangerous
her snake medicine, anti-venom
a trance-inducer who
sails on a crescent bay
brings wisdom from the depths
and fish into nets

oracular voices can still be heard
in the walls of the Sibyl's cave
alive and wild
is the sacred temple we live in
can never be tamed

ruins remain under the altar
where we unearth her frequency
in trees of laurel, oak and dark cedar
we crown her effigy with
rose garlands under waves

at night, she calls to us in dreams
when Sirius rises
the sirens sing

Venus Clam

vongole
devouring mouth
nape of the little neck

some see vulva
on the half shell
where Venus was born

innocuous eye
fornicata, quietly yawns
quivering steam

ready for wine to
further loosen *veritas*
from a yearning mouth

cool bath
of lemon cocktail
calms the fever

I prefer the heated sigh
pull of flesh
    pauses
suddenly decides
to release itself from
the prong of your fingers

rare and curious shell
where love enters
but may not return

veracious spawn of life
emerges from internal
licking tongues

Calamari 67

some nights we dream
    of a squid in a guitar
strumming love music
    tickling tentacles
around the belly of a woman
moving in and out of her
sensual talisman
of the invisible world
at moments, a *cornicello*
a number we play
upon a body of water
constantly dancing

often we pray
    at the foot of curves
    at the base of pleasures
siren songs lift us from depths
where squid hide
    in cerulean currents
to pull down a ship
or torpedo across waves
may only swim at night
    descend in arrows
    dodge spears and hooks
    dance under moonglow

how can we believe
we are more powerful
    than *calamari*
whose body holds the pen
who scribes
its own poems in blood
blackened trails erupt
upon those who want to
restrict his freedom to wander

he may hide
    in the grotto of her heart
she may plunge
    deeper than we can fathom
he may cover himself
    in a batter of kisses
she may sing in tide pools
    of oil and lemon
he may sacrifice himself
    into wedding rings
    for lips and tongues
she may write herself
    into poems and songs
he may flex his muscle
    of chameleon colors

a glassy eye scans for love
at high speed on high seas
three hearts pounding

Sea Urchin

he pulled up a spiny circle
a thousand needles on his palm
    I shall not touch it
I know what a broken heart feels like

I float backwards
illusion of independence
we share breath
swim in the same water
need each other

no one tells the sea urchin
that it's too clingy
there are no self-help books
no philosophies
the only therapy
that exists for anxious fish
is the sea anemone waving
pink fingers to swim inside for refuge

I'm unsure how the sea turtle
returns to the same beach it was born
navigates miles in a distant odyssey
dodges disaster, near misses with death
when it returns
does it feel the way I feel
home is an evolving place
never the same as I remember it
everywhere, a foreign land

is this why
the sea urchin clings to your hand
my breath an audible wave
sound and movement undulates
I search for your hand
I turn myself in circles
looking for you
    for myself underwater
with nothing left to cling to
no way of navigation

Consider the Oyster

androgynous hermit
sucking the open sea
clinging loneliness
filtered sorrow
between its lips
where foreign imperfections
spin an iridescent pearl
between its shell
twist darkness
into light
buries itself
in the muck
marinates in seaweed
sauce of tender pulp
licking flesh
amorphous
and vulnerable
fillets its talking mouth
into a brutal
open splice
raw with a quivering sigh
on its quick
dancing tongue
spiced with peppered citrus
may kiss you
taste you in return
the dripping
slippery ocean
slides
down
your
throat

Il Pesce

I return to baptize myself
in the aqueous salt of love

a fish out of water
unfolding scales of my tale
pour accordion centuries

I don't know if I can save you
reclined upon a silver platter
but I listen while
I compose poetic sermons

let me convert you into pleasure
sacrifice my twitching limbs
separate like loaves

ocean veins swim
propelled by moonlight
moving constellations
I can't help my blue nature

for you, I will run across water
hoist my eyes over waves
sprout wings that carry me
crashing into the deep

awash upon turquoise shallows
I'll kneel upon the sand
the mandorla of my body
a luminous glory

I'll turn over every shell
until I find the god
that listens to my prayers

Branzino

when I want to impress you I cook *branzino*
with his fins intact
his eyes still gazing at you

perhaps you think I'm cruel
as I open his mouth with my fingers
make him sing to you

you didn't hear
I named him *Giovanni*
baptized him
he multiplied to feed the masses

you didn't see
I massaged him with olive oil
filled him with lemon and thyme

when he arrives on the platter you say
how beautiful he is
decorated with capers and pepper
a king from the sea

he can say
what everyone longs to hear
that he was truly
loved

Reasons
to Return

Adrift

a fish flung ashore
gasps for air on Brooklyn asphalt
where small hands hold
hot rails of Gravesend Bay
look past the Atlantic
will long for home
never belong to one

one day I will venture where you left
roofs torn apart by bombs
buildings buried by lava
looking for a home
that does not exist
can never be found again

at the port
on streets full of ashes
the octopus
looks for an escape route
a crack inside a wall
where a sliver of sky shines

a looking glass sea ponders
the face of the moon
a city beneath a city
cobblestone chatters
footsteps of ghosts
men with eyes like grandpa
in markets full of sardines
the glassy eyes of the cod
pierce your soul

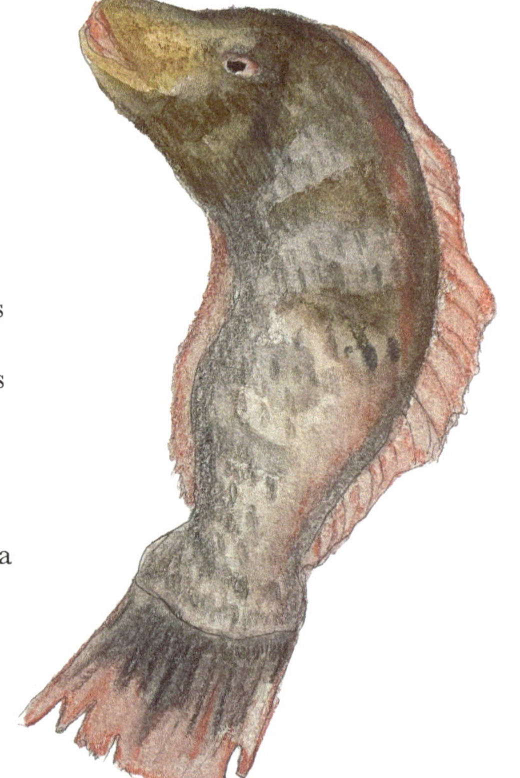

Marina Piccola

I blame spring
such heat carried into evening
when the edge of summer
caressed its shoulder
we whipped around
the curves of the island
past Madonna in her
illuminated grotto

the sunset, hot red
the first light of
Orion's belt appeared
after the tourists went home

you held me
barefoot on talking pebbles
wooden boats gently knocked
in the heaving sigh of swells
your warm hand
traveled between my shoulders

I unraveled my body
to enter moonlit waves
beyond the *Faraglioni*
with closed eyes
I walked across the bottom of the sea
returned to blue grottos

an ancient shore remembers
where I emerged
waters of my blood and island bones
my hips grew iridescent scales at dawn
and feet, fins
kept me here
in a silent song of longing
on a hot southern wind

Reasons to Return

because my grandfather's ghost
paces under grandma's balcony at night

miracles want to happen even if we don't believe
statues need our prayers and candles need lighting

we need to fall in love when our hearts are shattered
we don't know where our home is
    except in each other's eyes

so the angels don't get bored watching over us
our dreams must get a break from dreaming of elsewhere

volcanic soil is aching to grow us back to life again
seeds need somewhere to be planted
    tears need somewhere to fall

a lemon flower blossoms on a lonely hill
    and wants me to smell it
a deep ache asks me to change my eyes

your body by the window will look so good at sunset
my eyes long for a deep, Tyrrhenian blue

the sea misses my body, wants my body back
loneliness follows me down paths to sea caves

making love would feel delicious in a different bed
near a different window, with an expansive landscape

I want you in another language
I'm coming, but I don't know where I'm going

the pizza dough is being proofed
the only proof that we're alive is we are hungry

my soul needs at least one gelato,
     every afternoon, in a different flavor
we're both lost and need to forget ourselves

the balcony I stand on
     is waiting for you to serenade me
you come a little closer
     when we're in unfamiliar territory

if not you, then God in the form of songbirds
we are made of at least 60% water
     and the moon pulls us together

I'm restless now
     I said it's time
there does not need to be a reason

I dreamed of this
this is what I will remember

Apri la Bocca

open your mouth, she said
when you speak Italian

I can't find the words
language fails me
there is no translation for longing
I unlearn my shame

speak louder, with gusto
la bella lingua is fast
troppo veloce
my heart feels slow
heavy with sorrow

I use my hands when
I can't find the words
search for meaning
reach into the void
it's hard to express
this wandering nature

a distinct vibration
recreates my cells
even language
does not understand

musical phrases
with special rhythm
to learn to dance you must
step on your own toes

it's a romance language
I'm trying to speak
in a heartless place
afraid of love

who knows where it leads
it rambles up hillsides
scrambles down rivers
a current you must follow
a point leads to caverns
where land meets the sea

the waves have their language
cliffs are conversing
birds and wind whistle
herbs and flowers
sing in my blood

apri la bocca
allow the world to enter
soundless movements speak
body of earth, blood of sea

apri il tuo cuore

Gabish

when the poet says
     tawk and *cawfy*
my heart warms
to the sound of those words
as if I met an old friend
who recognizes me
in this place of no belonging

they washed
those words from my mouth
shoved missing letters
on the end of my words
asked me to place my tongue
at the top of my palette and repeat
     Take the time to talk to Tony
  not
     Take da time ta tawk to Tony

It's taken a lifetime
to know who I am
or what I'd say to Tony
the name of my Uncle
     I wanna speak
     a language we both don' feel
     embarrassed ta understand, ya know

my father used to say
     I don't speak Italian,
     I speak Brooklynese
mixed-up words
Southern Italian dialects and English
heavy sounds countered
rolling, sing-song Italian
I was never taught
I struggle hard to learn now

we are like those words
jumbled with our own sign language

only my hands truly understand me
a romantic curve
shoved into a sharpened box
in the name of survival

I try to learn my native tongue
to speak with ancestors in dreams
but it does not exist anymore

when my grandmother would ask me
    gabish itali-an?
I was instructed to reply
    no gabish, no gabish

how badly I want to *gabish,* now
    gabish Itali-an

I drift further from myself
a siren washed upon dry land
gills heaving from exhaustion

where is my song
that moves like water
if I were to sing it
what language would it be
    non Italiano, not dialect
a lost language of longing

can you see me from the shore
waving my hands
    gabish, gabish
sounds like waves
hitting the side of a boat
lapping onto black sand

Lemon Thief

if you gave me
a square foot of soil
baked by the sun
I'd plant a lemon tree

I trust my blood would know
the instructions by heart
like I trust my fingers to know
the right amount
of salt and herb for sauce

I don't measure life inch by inch
but by intuition

I long to grow a seed
watch a vine spring forth
an erubescent planet
to walk into a backyard
instead of a corner store
to pluck sprigs of basil
with my own hands
to make a dish
with more love

for now
my heart breaks
every time I pass a lemon tree
behind a fence
just out of reach

Notes

Notes

Page 4 & 5, **Sirenland & dell'Ovo** – Both sides of my family
come from towns along the flanks of Mount Vesuvius in the
Bay of Naples, Italy—an area once part of ancient Greece
and deeply tied to the mythology of the sirens. Most famously
featured in Homer's *Odyssey*, the sirens were believed to inhabit
the rocky coves along Sorrento and Amalfi Coast. Though
once considered dangerous to men, their image evolved into
protective symbols—guardians of fishermen, ports, and guides
for souls in transition.

Temples honoring the sirens once stood on the Sorrento
peninsula and in Naples. The death of the siren Partenope, after
the *Odyssey*, is said to be the origin story of Naples: her body
washed ashore in the area now called Santa Lucia, and from
it, the city of Partenope was born—its people, originally called
Partenopeans.

Another legend tells of the poet Virgil finding Partenope's egg,
which he enchanted to protect the city; that egg is believed
to still reside within Castel dell'Ovo ("Castle of the Egg"),
safeguarding Naples from volcanic eruptions. Symbols of the
sirens appear on ancient pottery, gravesites, and protective home
chimes. Originally depicted as part-woman, part-bird, with
wings—sirens gradually evolved into the half-fish forms we
now associate with mermaids.

Page 8 & 18, **Corallini & Rosa** – My grandparents on my
father's side came from Torre del Greco ("Greek Tower") near
Naples, known as the City of Flowers and Coral. Once a hub
for coral harvesting, the town is still renowned for its expert

craftsmanship in carving coral and carnelian shells into cameos, beads, and intricate works of art. Locals were called "Corallini" for this tradition. My grandmother, Rosa, hand-carved cameos, and I'm lucky to have one she made, illustrated here—both cherished heirlooms. The town also cultivates flowers on farms along the slopes of Mount Vesuvius. Further south lies the ancient site of Paestum, called the City of Roses, home to some of the best-preserved Greek temples in the region, including sanctuaries to Hera and Athena. There, damask roses—specifically the Paestum Rose—were once grown and distilled into oils and fragrances used in rituals and blessings.

Page 21, **The Mourners** – Hired mourners, known as "Le Prefiche," were a longstanding funeral tradition in Southern Italy, including at my grandfather's funeral. The practice dates back to ancient Greece and possibly Egypt, and may be linked to the mythology of the sirens—especially through the use of song in mourning. These women sang about the deceased and expressed intense emotion through wailing and weeping. Sirens were often depicted on graves as spirit guardians and guides for the soul's passage.

Page 23, **What to Do with Your Tears** – Alchemists used glass bottles for distillation and storage of volatile chemicals in their experiments with transmutations. Glass bottles called "Lachrymatory" bottles, often made of glass or terracotta, found in Greek and Roman era tombs, were formerly believed to hold the tears of mourners. Legend suggests the bottles were sealed and kept until the tears evaporated, signaling the end of mourning.

Page 33, **L'occhio** – (the eye) is short for "malocchio" (the evil eye) which remains a prevalent folk belief in Naples. It's thought that an envious look or thought—intentional or not—can cause misfortune, harm, or even illness. Protective customs include wearing "il corno" (the horn), traditionally made of silver, coral, or ceramic and always given as a gift, as well as using "la mano cornuta" ("the horned hand") or simply "le corna" ("the horns") hand gesture when no amulet is available. Ancient healers performed rituals to remove "malocchio" using olive oil and water. The horn symbol may trace back to goddess imagery, such as the bull or cornucopia.

Page 35, **Matermania** – On the island of Capri lies a beautiful cavern that was once a sacred site for worshipping the goddess Cybele (Magna Mater), brought from Anatolia to Italy by Roman prophecy from the Sibyl of Cumae—one of the earliest Greek settlements in the Bay of Naples. The Sibyls delivered their prophecies in poetic verse. The cavern, once home to hypnotic rituals for Cybele and a shrine to water nymphs due to its ancient spring, occasionally hosts secret sunrise concerts known mostly to locals.

Page 36, **Nymphaeum** – Nymphs were guardians of sacred water sources, and a "nymphaeum" was a sanctuary dedicated to their worship. In ancient Greece, gratitude offerings—often elaborate ex-votos (Latin for "from a vow," referring to an offering left in a sacred place to fulfill a promise or express gratitude for a miracle) carved in marble or stone—were left to commemorate healings at these sites.

Page 37, **Secret Cabinet** – Il Gabinetto Segreto is a section of rooms in the Naples Archeological museum that houses erotic art found in the sites of Pompeii and Herculaneum. Originally censored due to their sexual nature and requiring a special ticket to view them, they are now open to viewing.

Page 42, **Genius Loci** – Latin for "spirit of the place," in Roman times, the "Genius Loci" was the protective, guardian spirit of sacred places in nature, such as a natural spring or meadow, often honored with a temple or shrine. The word "genius," comes from this concept. "Genius Loci" can also reference the distinctive atmosphere, character or feeling of a place.

Page 51, **Calamari 67** – The Squid in the Guitar is a symbol from *La Smorfia Napoletana,* a Neapolitan book of divination where each symbol corresponds to a number. The name "La Smorfia" may derive from Morpheus, the Greek god of dreams. Traditionally used to interpret dreams, "La Smorfia" also applies to symbols encountered in waking life—on the street, in songs, films, or news stories. Repeated symbols are seen as auspicious, and their numbers are used in lottery play, turning it into a kind of common spiritual practice. "The Squid in the Guitar, Number 67," is thought to symbolize a sexual or creative act.

Page 54, **Consider the Oyster** – the title of this poem is taken from the famous book, *Consider the Oyster,* by MFK Fisher which explores the history, preparation, and enjoyment of oysters. Often considered an aphrodisiac food.

Mille Grazie

Thank you to the following organizations and publications in which these poems have been published:

"Nymphaeum," *Colossus: Current – The Ways and Workings of Water, Colossus Press,* June 2025

"What Do the Stars Look Like in the Middle of the Ocean," *Forum, Literary Magazine of CCSF,* December 2018

"Consider the Oyster," *Marin Poetry Center Anthology,* September 2018

Heartfelt gratitude and loving recognition to the Ramaytush Ohlone and Coastal Miwok peoples on the unceded lands of the San Francisco Bay.

To my family in the United States and Italy for reconnecting me to our ancestors and their stories—I continue to listen with deep reverence.

Thank you to Cara Gardner, Gail Faith Edwards, and Kara Wood, for sharing tools to access the wisdom of my ancestors—human, animal, elemental, mythic and cosmic—that sing through this book.

To Ingrid Keir and Feather Press for bringing her editorial craft to these poems, for her guiding fire to bring this book to life, and for her epic friendship on this journey and always.

To Daniel Heffez for his encouragement, patience and willingness to travel with me on many deep and wild journeys into Sirenland.

Grazie to my Italian teacher Valentina Ottiano for refining and expanding my skills to converse and therefore to reconnect.

To the Museo Archeologico Nazionale di Napoli, Ministero della Cultura, and the Getty Villa, for their support and for the preservation of the art featured in these poems.

Deep appreciation to the Italian and Italian-American cultural institutions in North Beach, San Francisco—especially Joseph Carboni at Libreria Pino and Telegraph Hill Books, Franca Cavallaro & Beatrice Penni at Istituto Italiano di Cultura di San Francisco, Sandra Bagnatori, Susan Filippo and Bianca Friundi at Museo Italo Americano, Tony Gemignani at Giovanni's, the SF Italian Athletic Club, and Consolato Generale d'Italia San Francisco—for their support.

To Agneta Falk Hirschman and Anna Lombardo for their guidance and for including me in the poetry community at the International Poetry Festival in Venezia. To my Italian and Italian-American artists: Alexandria Giardino, Giuseppe Pinto, Giovanni Liguoro at Poesia Cafe, Sara Marinelli, Tommi Avicolli Mecca, Bear Toffoli, Diego DeLeo & Gianmaria Franchini for dreaming and co-creating ecstatic poetry rituals with me.

Mille grazie to the support of my local poetry community: to Genny Lim & SF Jazz, Andrew Paul Nelson, Caitlyn Skye Wild and friends at Golden Sardine, Jessica Loos & Dan Macchiarini, The Beat Museum, Bird & Beckett Books, Dan Brady at Sacred Grounds, Clara Hsu at Clarion Arts and the wonderful Kim Shuck for featuring these poems at Fire Thieves, Poem Jam, and many more with support from, and much gratitude to John Smalley and friends at the San Francisco Public Library, Main Branch and Richard Le at North Beach Branch Library.

Lastly, many thanks to the Mill Valley Public Library where this book was developed while looking out at the redwood trees and dreaming of the Tyrrhenian Sea.

Jennifer Barone

Jennifer is an Italian-American poet and artist, born in Brooklyn, New York, with roots in the Bay of Naples, Italy. She is the author of four poetry collections and the creator of the artwork featured in this book.

A two-time winner of the San Francisco Public Library's *Poets Eleven* contest for North Beach, where Jennifer resides— a neighborhood known for its Italian heritage and a lineage of poets and artists. At Libreria Pino and Telegraph Hill Books, she curates and hosts Italian-English poetry readings, leads writing workshops, and hosts the *Voices From the Hill* podcast, interviewing SF Bay Area authors at telhilit.org/podcast.

Her work has been published in multiple literary journals, and featured at *LitQuake, SFMOMA, de Young Museum, SF Public Library, Marin Poetry Center, Petaluma Poetry Walk,* and the *SF Jazz Poetry and Jazz Festival,* among others.

Deeply inspired by her travels, she studies Italian and her writing workshops blend Italian culture with metaphysical and alchemical themes. Beyond writing, she is a graphic designer, teaches yoga, and offers energy work and sound healing through innerlotus.com. She also collects vintage typewriters and loves composing spontaneous poems at special events on her Ferrari-red Olivetti.

Visit: **jenniferbarone.wordpress.com**
Instagram: **@baronejenn**

Also by Jennifer Barone:

Saporoso, Poems of Italian Food & Love
    with artwork by Lam Khong

Secret City
    with artwork by Edward Barone

Simple Language

About Feather Press

Feather Press is an independent literary press dedicated
to uplifting the voices of local poets, writers, and artists.
We believe in creative abundance—that every individual
carries a deep well of story, history, and lineage waiting
to be expressed. Guided by a commitment to cultural
and racial diversity, we support both emerging and
established voices with care and intention.

Through publications and community gatherings,
Feather Press creates space for connection, celebration,
and the shared power of story. We publish work that is
honest, radiant, and real—work that refuses to shrink
in a world asking us to harden.

Feather Press Titles:

The Tender Hearts Club, Volume One, An Anthology of Love Poems,
Edited by Ingrid Keir

Saporoso, Poems of Italian Food & Love,
by Jennifer Barone with artwork by Lam Khong

The Choreography of Nests,
by Ingrid Keir

To learn more about our publications and upcoming events,
visit **featherpressbooks.wordpress.com**